LESLEY COLGAN M.Sc.

T H E

FLAVONOID REVOLUTION

GRAPE SEED EXTRACT AND OTHER FLAVONOIDS AGAINST DISEASE

APPLE PUBLISHING

ISBN 1–896817–05–X

Apple Publishing Company Ltd.
220 East 59th Avenue
Vancouver, British Columbia
Canada v5x 1x9
Tel (604) 214-6688 • Fax (604) 214-3566

CONTENTS

THE FLAVONOID REVOLUTION

GRAPE SEED EXTRACT AND OTHER FLAVONOIDS AGAINST DISEASE

Thousands of years ago our ancestors were hunter-gatherers. They ate a wide variety of plants and seeds. Today our diet has reversed. We eat too much meat, too much fat and too few plants. Our diet is now missing the large numbers of plant flavonoids and other phytochemicals that we evolved to use.

As science has begun to realize their importance in our diet and our health, plant phytochemicals including flavonoids and carotenoids have come under close scrutiny. The problem is the large numbers of these nutrients. The number of known flavonoids in plants is over 20,000, and only 4,000 have been chemically analysed or tested. Of these 4,000, about 100 have been researched thoroughly. Each one we do research, further confirms the wisdom of eating a wide variety of fruits and vegetables.

Flavonoids are a class of nutrients that form part of a broader family of aromatic compounds called "polyphenols". Plants make these polyphenols from the amino acid phenylalanine and acetate. Flavonoids are responsible for many of the brilliant colors that you see in fruits and vegetables, and are the source of the astringent or tannic tastes of green tea, dry red wines and many herbs.

Known flavonoids can be categorized into nine classes based on their chemical characteristics as shown in Table 1. They are potent antioxidants and have a wide array of biochemical functions. They are involved in immune function, gene expression, capillary and cerebral blood flow, platelet aggregation, liver function, enzyme activity, and collagen, phospholipid, cholesterol and histamine metabolism.[1-3]

Table 1:
Flavonoid classes based on chemical characterizations

Flavonoid Class	Class Members	Plant Sources
Flavanols	Catechins	Green tea, grape seeds, pine bark
Proanthocyanidins	Oligomeric catechins	Pine bark, grape seeds, leaves of bilberry, birch, ginkgo biloba
Flavones & flavonols	Quercetin, kaempferol	Apples, green tea, ginkgo leaves, grape skins, milk thistle fruits
Biflavones	Amentoflavone, bilobetin	Ginkgo leaves
Flavanones	Hesperidin, naringin	Citrus peels
Flavanonoles	Taxifolin	Milk thistle fruits, pine bark
Anthocyanins, Anthocyanidins & Anthocyanosides	Cyanidin, delphinidin, malvidin, petunidin	red and black grapes, red wine, bilberries
Flavonolignans	Silymarin	Milk thistle fruits, artichokes
Isoflavones	Genistein, diadzein	Soy beans

FLAVONOIDS AGAINST HEART DISEASE

Clinical research has clearly documented the role of free radical damage in the progression of numerous degenerative diseases, particularly cardiovascular disease (and certain forms of cancer). Research shows the heart is receptive to the benefits of targeted phytonutrients, antioxidants and nutritionals. Studies have concluded that the combination of a healthy diet supplemented with antioxidants and phytonutrients may be useful in the prevention and promotion of optimum cardiovascular health.[4]

A recent study reported in the **British Medical Journal** was undertaken in Finland between 1967 and 1992 on 5,133 Finnish men and women aged 30–69 years and free from heart disease at the beginning of the study. The study concluded that people with very low intakes of flavonoids were at higher risk of coronary heart disease.[5] A long term study undertaken on 34,789 male health professionals concluded that intake of flavonoids does have a protective effect in men with established coronary heart disease.[6]

Another large trial, the Zutphen study, investigated the relationship between flavonoid intake and incidence of stroke. The study began in 1970 and ran for 15 years on 552 men aged 50 to 69 years. Dietary flavonoids (mainly quercetin) were inversely associated with stroke incidence after adjustment for potential confounders, including other antioxidant vitamins.[7] Another recent study concluded that flavonoids also inhibit lipid peroxidation at microsomal level in the heart and therefore are cardioprotective against this specific type of oxidation.[8]

Flavonoids work with and enhance the effects of other antioxidants as well. A study by Mathiesen and colleagues showed that lipid peroxidation in LDL cholesterol can be slowed down more by combining flavonoids and vitamin C, than by either one alone.[9]

FLAVONOIDS AGAINST DEGENERATIVE DISEASES

Body cells and tissues are threatened continuously by damage caused by free radicals and reactive oxygen species produced during normal oxygen metabolism, as well as by toxic agents in the environment and other chemical reactions. Free radicals are capable of disrupting metabolic activity and cell structure. When this occurs, additional free radicals are produced, which can result in more extensive damage to cells and tissues. We know now that the uncontrolled production of free radicals is thought to be a major contributing factor to many degenerative diseases.[10]

Flavonoids are able to capture and neutralize excessive free radicals in many tissues of the body. They work in synergy with the other antioxidant vitamins such as vitamins C and E. Many flavonoids are also capable of binding to metal ions, which prevents those metals from acting as catalysts in the body that enhance free radical production. Some flavonoids also help regulate activity of the body's own antioxidant enzymes, superoxide dismutase (SOD) and glutathione peroxidase.[10]

FLAVONOIDS AGAINST CANCER

There has been many studies showing that intakes of flavonoids can help prevent cancer. Brilliant researcher Dr. Gladys Block and colleagues at the University of California, Berkeley analyzed all 170 of the controlled studies up to 1992, on effects of fruit and vegetables on cancer.[11]

Some examples from their analysis:

Type of Cancer	No. of studies showing protection.
Lung cancer	24
Colo-rectal cancer	20
Stomach cancer	17
Esophageal cancer	15
Oral cancer	9
Cervical cancer	7

And on and on and on. We are now certain that flavonoids obtained by eating copious amounts of fruits and vegetables, can protect you against most types of cancer.[12] In fact, nutrition science is slowly realizing that many of these compounds may be essential to maintain optimal health.

The recommended intake of fruit and vegetables is four to five servings a day. Dr. Gladys Block and colleagues at the National Cancer Institute completed a survey showing that Americans actually eat, on average, less than one serving a day of either fruit or vegetables (potatoes and lettuce excluded).[13]

According to the National Cancer Institute (NCI), approximately 35% of all cancer cases may be directly caused by poor diet. In contrast, close to 200 epidemiological studies show that there is a lower risk of many types of cancers among those who eat large quantities of fruits and vegetables. The NCI is currently sponsoring a major effort to identify the biological activity of various phytochemicals, including flavonoids, in the hope that detailed dietary guidelines designed to achieve specific disease-prevention goals can be established.

TYPES AND SOURCES OF FLAVONOIDS: RED & WHITE GRAPES

Proanthocyanidins from pine bark and grapes have an interesting history, and are the longest studied of all the flavonoids. Proanthocyanidins and their antioxidant activities were discovered by Professor Jacques Masquelier of the University of Bordeaux, France. In 1948 Professor Masquelier discovered that peanuts containing procyanidolic oligomers (PCO's) increased the strength of blood vessels in laboratory animals.[14]

He heard the story about the famous French explorer Jacques Cartier, who had been introduced to a tea made from the bark and leaves of a large pine tree that grew in the area of Canada's Gulf of St Lawrence. He began research on the bark of a similar tree, the maritime pine that grows in the southern regions of France. After extensive research he patented an extraction process in 1951. Proanthocyanidins from pine bark extracted using Professor Masquelier's process are sold under the name Pycnogenol". Then in 1970, he patented a second extraction process, this time for proanthocyanidins from grape seeds, which he calls Grapenol". Professor Masquelier's research has confirmed the structure, effects and lack of toxicity of these sources of proanthocyanidins.[15,16]

Camellia sinensis

PROANTHOCYANIDINS AND CAPILLARY HEALTH

The proanthocyanidins found in grape seeds and pine bark, as well as the anthocyanosides of bilberries and flavanones in citrus peel have been recognized for many decades to support the capillary system. Their presence in the capillary vessel basement membranes and surrounding collagen structures is responsible for maintaining proper capillary permeability and stability. Healthy resilient capillary vessels, rich in proanthocyanidins, maintain their shape and function for normal, efficient microcirculation and prevent water accumulation in the surrounding tissues.

PROANTHOCYANIDINS AND BLOOD CLOTS

Studies show proanthocyanidins stop platelets becoming sticky, and maintain blood vessel elasticity, which can aid in keeping blood pressure down.[17,18,19] Studies show the anthocyanins which come from the skins of red grapes helps prevent the detrimental oxidation of blood lipoproteins such as LDL cholesterol.[20]

Recent studies also show that drinking wine has a protective effect against heart disease. It is believed to be the proanthocyanidins and other flavonoids in the grapes that provide these protective effects.[20]

PROANTHOCYANIDINS AND CONNECTIVE TISSUE

Your connective tissue is the mesh that holds your body together. In infants it is smooth and elastic. But these tissues slowly oxidize and become cross-linked and rigid with age, losing their elasticity. Studies show that flavonoids in grape seeds bind to the glycosaminoglycans, collagen and elastin, protecting them from oxidation and inflammatory damage. And, when combined with vitamin C, grape seed extract enhances the biosynthesis of new collagen and elastin.[21,22]

PROANTHOCYANIDINS AGAINST INFLAMMATION AND ALLERGIES

Proanthocyanidins also selectively bind to connective tissue of joints, preventing swelling, healing damaged tissue, and lessening pain.[3,23] They also show anti-inflammatory effects by inhibiting the release and synthesis of certain compounds that promote inflammation, such as histamine, serine protease, prostaglandins and leukotrienes.[1,2,23]

The anti-histamine action of proanthocyanidins is mediated by an inhibiting effect on the enzyme **histidine decarboxylase** which is responsible for the production of histamine. This is enhanced by proanthocyanidins ability to block **hyaluronidase**, the enzyme that facilitates the release of histamine into body tissues. This effect causes proanthocyanidins to have strong anti-allergic action in many people. As well as its anti-histamine effect it also strengthens cell membranes of basophils and mast cells which can contain the allergic chemicals thus preventing the hypersensitivity.[2,24,25,26]

A related substance in grapes called resveratrol (not a flavonoid) has been the subject of recent investigation as a cancer chemopreventive. Scientists reported recently that resveratrol acted as an antioxidant and antimutagen and blocked other cell-changing agents from causing cancerous changes in cells.[27]

Suggested Daily Dose: A combination of 100–200 mg of pine bark and grape seed extract, yielding 85–92% proanthocyanidins; and 50–100 mg of red grape skin extract yielding 30% anthocyanins.

BILBERRY FOR YOUR EYES

The bilberry (*Vaccinium myrtillus*), a northern European cousin of the North American blueberry, has been surrounded by folklore for centuries for its many benefits. During World War II, British RAF pilots would eat bilberry jam on bread shortly before their night raids to improve night vision. Their bombing accuracy was far greater than that of German pilots, though whether this was due to bilberry is unknown. Bilberry's other family members also include the lowbush blueberry, cranberry and lingonberry. All these species contain anthocyanosides, but bilberry is the most common form found in supplements.

We all fear loss of our eyesight as much as we fear loss of our intellect. The sun's ultraviolet radiation can cause free-radical damage to the lens and retina of the eye. As the proteins in your lens oxidze, they form a thickened lens known as a cataract that eventually obscures vision. Age-related macular degeneration is another serious eye condition that afflicts more and more people.

In one study anthocyanosides from bilberry extract plus vitamin E, stopped the progression of cataract formation in 97% of patients tested.[28] In clinical trials of patients with various types of retinal disease, those who were given flavonoids have shown significant improvement.[29,30,31]

The anthocyanosides in bilberries is a potent antioxidant and is found to be important for eye health and normal wound healing.[32] Bilberries also seem to aid in protection against ulcers and in the healing process by binding to the connective tissue of the mucosal membranes.[33]

Anthocyanosides have been recognized for many decades to support the capillary system. Their presence in the capillary vessel basement membranes and surrounding collagen structures is responsible for maintaining proper capillary permeability and stability.[34] Healthy and resilient capillary vessels are able to maintain their shape and function for normal, efficient microcirculation to prevent water accumulation in the surrounding tissues.

Suggested Daily Dose: A bilberry extract of 120–240 mg yielding 25% anthocyanosides.

GREEN TEA FOR YOUR HEART

Green tea (*Camellia sinensis*) is one of the most widely consumed beverages in the world. The Chinese and Japanese typically consume 2 to 10 cups of green tea daily.

Polyphenolic catechins from green tea help maintain healthy blood cholesterol levels and prevent thrombosis formation.[35] A recent study completed in Japan examined the relationship between green tea consumption and serum cholesterol and low density lipoproteins (LDL), in 2,062 male self-defense officials. They found that green tea consumption was inversely associated with serum cholesterol levels and LDL ratios.[36] Black tea loses its beneficial catechins due to fermentation.

The polyphenolic catechins in green tea also have marked antimutagenic potential.[37,38] It also seems to inhibit infection by the influenza virus as well as having an anti-bacterial effect on *Streptococcus*.[39,40]

Suggested Daily Dose: A green tea extract of 500–900 mg, yielding 20% polyphenols.

MILK THISTLE FOR YOUR LIVER

Milk thistle (*silybum marianum*) is a Mediterranean plant producing fruits that are rich in a group of flavonoids known collectively as silymarin. Today's exposure to environmental pollution through our environment, places extra demands on the liver's antioxidant defense and detoxifying systems.

Silymarin has been shown to support healthy liver function under a variety of environmental stress factors such as alcohol consumption, exposure to pollutants and harmful viruses and bacteria.[41,42]

In a recent study, silymarin was found to protect liver and skin cells from drug induced toxicity under controlled conditions.[43] In another study, researchers tested the hepatoprotective (liver protective) effects of silymarin on rats exposed to radiation. The effects of the silymarin was evaluated after looking at the changes in the nucleic acids in the liver, spleen and bone marrow. It was found that the nucleic acid changes in irradiated rats were alleviated by the post-radiation application of silymarin.[44]

Suggested Daily Dose: A standardized milk thistle extract of 150–200 mg, yielding 80% silymarin.

SOYBEANS AGAINST CANCER

A recent study looked at the effects of the isoflavone **genistein** from soybeans. The researchers concluded that genistein has strong antioxidant and antiproliferative effects giving it a strong anticarcinogenic effect.[45]

It is found in high concentration in soybeans and has high bioavailablity making it an important candidate for cancer prevention.

Suggested Daily Dose: Currently there are no soybean extracts available in supplement form.

GINKGO BILOBA FOR YOUR BRAIN

Known in traditional Chinese medicine for about 5,000 years. Ginkgo is a tree that grows over 100 ft tall and is extremely slow growing. Specimens can live for 2,000 to 4,000 years. It is the oldest tree known to man. Ginkgo contains beneficial flavonoids as flavone glycosides and the non-flavonoid compounds of terpene lactones which are another important non-flavonoid phytochemical.

Ginkgo has long been known to influence capillary and cerebral microcirculation.[46,47] In animal studies it has been shown to increase cerebral blood flow and oxygen consumption in the brain.[48] In one study of human subjects, intravenous administration of ginkgo increased blood flow by up to 70%.[49] Ginkgo has also been used successfully in treatment of a variety of conditions involving vascular insufficiency and obstructive arterial syndrome including Raynaud's disease, post phlebitis syndrome and peripheral vascular disorders.[50,51]

Clastogenic factors are found in the plasma of persons who have been exposed to radiation both accidentally and therapeutically.

A clastogen is anything that causes chromsome damage. These clastogenic factors have been found in the plasma of Chernobyl accident recovery workers. A recently reported study treated 30 of these workers with ginkgo biloba extract.

After two months of supplementation the clastogenic activity was reduced to control levels. After cessation of treatment a follow-up over one year showed the benefit of the treatment persisted for at least seven months. The study demonstrates that continuous supplementation could protect against the clastogenic effects of radiation exposure.[52]

Suggested Daily Dose: A standardized extract of 50–100 mg of ginkgo biloba yielding 24% flavone glycosides.

CITRUS FRUITS FOR YOUR CIRCULATION

Because of the wide-spread popularity of citrus fruits, citrus biioflavonoids account for the great majority of our total daily flavonoid intake. The white albedo layer of citrus peel is especially rich in the bitter tasting flavanones hesperidin and naringin. Citrus juices, however, are low in bioflavonoids. Like most flavonoids, those from citrus are free radical scavenging antioxidants that work in synergy with vitamin C.

The flavanones in citrus peel have long been recognized for many decades to support the capillary system. They help maintain proper capillary permeability and stability.[34]

Other studies have examined the antimutagenic properties of the citrus flavonoids **naringin, hesperidin, nobiletin and tangeretin**. The evidence indicates that these citrus flavonoids, especially tangeretin and nobiletin may play a role in the chemoprevention of cancer.[53]

Suggested Daily Dose: A mixed citrus bioflavonoid extract of 200–300 mg, yielding 50% active bioflavonoids.

FLAVONOIDS ARE SAFE

We hope the above sketch of some of the new research on flavonoids is enough to convince you of their importance for your health and longevity. We have been able to touch on only a few of the prominent findings. At the Colgan Institute our research base now numbers over 400 studies. Most have had positive findings of potent flavonoid effects against disease. The evidence is now so strong that flavonoids are quickly gaining the status of nutrients essential for normal health.

Being normal constituents of fruits and vegetables, they are literally as safe as Mom's apple pie. Use them with confidence as a valuable adjunct to your daily intake of vitamins and minerals. We advise you to use whenever possible, standardized extracts of these nutrients. The labels should state the percentage of active ingredient in the product. These products are more likely to contain active ingredients.

Michael Colgan, Lesley Colgan,
San Diego, California 1997

Ginkgo (Ginko Biloba)

REFERENCES

1. Gabor M. Pharmacologic effects of flavonoids on blood vessels. **Angiologica**, 1972;9:355-374.

2. Amella M, et al. Inhibition of mast cell histamine release by flavonoids and bioflavonoids. **Planta Medica** ,1985;5116-5120.

3. Rao CN, et al. Influence of flavonoids on the collagen metabolism in rats with adjuvant induced arthritis. **Ital J Biochem**, 1981;30:54-62.

4. Sinatra ST, DeMarco J. Free radicals, oxidative stress, oxidized low density lipoprotein (LDL) and the heart: antioxidants and other strategies to limit cardiovascular damage. **Conn Med**, 1995;59(10):579-88.

5. Knekt P, et al. Flavonoid intake and coronary mortality in Finland: a cohort study. **Brit Med J**, 1996;312(7029):478-81.

6. Rimm EB, et al. Relation between intake of flavonoids and risk for coronary heart disease in male health professionals. **Ann Intern Med**, 1996;125(5):384-9.

7. Keli SO, et al. Dietary flavonoids, antioxidant vitamins, and incidence of stroke: the Zutphen study. **Arch Intern Med**, 1996; 156(6):637-42.

8. Van Acker SA, et al. Structural aspects of antioxidant activity of flavonoids. **Free Radic Biol Med**, 1996;20(3):331-42.

9. Mathiesen L, et al. Inhibition of lipid peroxidation in low-density lipoprotein by the flavonoid myrigalone B and ascorbic acid. **Biochem Pharmacol**, 1996;51(12):1719-25.

10. Kitani K, et al (eds). **Pharmacological Intervention In Aging and Age-Associated Disorders.** New York:The New York Academy of Sciences, 1996.13. Block G, et al. **Amer J Epidemiol**, 1988;127:297.

11. Block G, et al. **Nutr and Cancer**, 1992;18:1-29.

12. Block G, et al. **Nutr & Cancer**, 1992;18:1-29.

13. Block G, et al. **Amer J Epidemiol**, 1988;127:297.

14. Masquelier J. Recherche sur les pigments de la graine d'arachide, these de doctoral es-sciences. Drouillard edit, Bordeaux, 1948.

15. Masquelier, J. Plant extract with a proanthocyanidin content as therapeutic agent having radical scavenging effect and use thereof. U.S. Patent No.4,698,360.

16. Masquelier J, Dumon MC, Dumas J. Stabilisation du collagen par des oligomeres procyanidoliques. **Acta Therapeutica**, 1981;7:101-105.

17. Largrue G, et al. A study of the effects of procyanidol oligomers on capillary resistance in hypertension and in certain nephropathies. **Sem Hop Paris**, 1981;57:1399-1401.

18. Detre A, et al. Studies on vascular permeability in hypertension: action of anthocyanosides. **Clin Physiol Biochem**, 1986;4:143-149.

19. Meunier MT, et al. Inhibition of angiotension I converting enzyme by flavanolic compounds: In vitro and in vivo studies. **Planta Medica**, 1987;54:12-15.

20. Fitzpatick DF, et al. Endothelium-dependent vasorelaxing activity of wine and other grape products. **Amer J Physiol,** 1993;9:105-113.

21. Masquelier J. Procyanidolic oligomers. **J Parfums Cosmet Arom,** 1990;95:889-97.

22. Hagerman AE, Butler LG. The specificity of proanthocyanidin-protein interactions. **J Biol Chem,** 1981;256:4494-4497.

23. Baruch J. Effect of Endotelon (95% PCO derived from grape seeds) in postoperative edema. Results of a double-blind study versus placebo in 32 female patients. **Ann Chir Plas Esthet,** 1984;29:393-395.

24. Laparra J. Pharmacokinetic study of the total procyanidolic oligomers of the grape. **Acta Therpeutica,** 1978;4:233-246.

25. Middleton E, Drzewieki G. Flavonoid inhibition of human basophil histamine release stimulated by various agents. **Biochem Pharmacol,** 1984;33:3333-3338.

26. Pearce F, et al. Mucosal mast cells. III. Effects of quercetin and other flavonoids on antigen-induced histamine secretion from rat intestinal mast cells. **J Allergy Clin Immunol,** 1984;73:819-823.

27. Jang M, et al. Cancer chemopreventive activity of resveratrol, a natural product derived from grapes. **Science,** 1997;275:218-219.

28. Bravetti G. Preventive medical treatment of senile cataract with vitamin E and anthocyanosides: Clinical evaluation. **Ann Opthalmol Clin Ocul,** 1989;115:109.

29. Saracco JB, Estachy GM. Etude de l'Endotelon enopthalmoligie. **Gaz Med de France,** 1981;88:2035-2038.

30. Scharrer A, Ober M. Anthocyanosides in the treatment of retinopathies. **Klin Monatsbl Augenheilkd**, 1981;178:386-389.

31. Corbe C, et al. Microangiopathy of the retina. **J Fr Opthalmol**, 1988;11:453.

32. Lietti A, et al. Studies on *Vaccinum myrtillus* anthocyanosides I. Vasoprotective and anti-inflammatory activity. **Arzneim Forsch**, 1976;26:829-832.

33. Magistretti MJ, et al. Anti-ulcer activity of an anthocyanidin from *Vaccinium myrtillus*. **Arzneim Forsch**, 1988;38:686-690.

34. Robert L, et al. Action of procyanidolic oligomers on vascular permeability. **Path Biol**, 1990;38:608-616.

35. Ali M, et al. A potent thromboxane formation inhibitor in green tea leaves. **Prostagl Leukotr Ess Fatty Acids**, 1990;40:281-283.

36. Kono S, et al. Relation of green tea consumption to serum lipids and lipoproteins in Japanese men. **J Epidemiol**, 1996;6(3):128-33.

37. Bu-Abbas A, et al. Marked antimutagenic potential of aqueous green tea extracts: mechanics of action. **Mutagenesis**, 1994;9:3250331.

38. Wang ZY, et al. Antimutagenic activity of green tea polyphenols. **Mutation Res**, 1989;223:273-285.

39. Nakayama M, et al. Inhibition of the infectivity of influenza virus by tea polyphenols. **Antiviral Res**, 1993;21:289-299.

40. Sakanaka S, et al. Antibacterial substances in Japanese green tea extract against *Streptoccus* mutans, a cariogenic bacterium. **Agric Biol Chem**, 1989;53:2307-2311.

41. Ferenci P, et al. Randomized controlled trial of silymarin treatment in patients with cirrhosis of the liver. **J Hepatol**, 1989;9:105-113.

42. Muzes G, et al. Effect of the bioflavonoid silymarin on the in-vitro activity and expression of superoxide dismutase (SOD) enzyme. **Acta Physiol Hung**, 1995;78:3-9.

43. Shear NH, et al. Acetaminophen-induced toxicity to human epidermoid cell line A431 and hepatoblastoma cell line Hep G2, in-vitro, is diminshed by silymarin. **Skin Pharmacol**, 1995;8(6):279-91.

44. Hakova H, Misurova E. Therpeutical effect of silymarin on nucleic acids in the various organs of rats after radiation injury. **Radiats Biol Radioecol**, 1996;36(3):365-70.

45. Wei H, et al. Antioxidant and antipromotional effects of the soybean isoflavone genistein. **Pro Soc Exp Biol Med**, 1995;208(1):124-30.

46. Hellegoarch A, et al. **Gen Pharmacol**, 1985;16:129.

47. Clostre F, DeFeudis FV. **Cardiovascular Effects of Ginkgo biloba Extract (EGB761)**, New York: Elsevier, 1995.

48. Lafitte M, et al. **Arch Int Pharmcodyn**, 1980;243:236.

49. Saponaro A. **Minerva Medica**, 1973;709:4194.

50. Nazzaro P, Dicarlo A. **Minerva Medica**, 1973;79:4198.

51. Bauer V. **Arnzeim Forsch**, 1984;34:716.

52. Emerit I, et al. Clastogenic factors in the plasma of Chernobyl accident recovery workers: anticlastogenic effect of Ginkgo biloba extract. **Radiat Res**, 1995;144(2):1998-2005.

53. Calomme M, et al. Inhibition of bacterial mutagenesis by Citrus flavonoids. **Planta Med**, 1996;62(3):222-6.